ALSO BY PAUL MULDOON

New Weather (1973)

Mules (1977)

Why Brownlee Left (1980)

Quoof (1983)

Meeting the British (1987)

Selected Poems 1968-1986 (1987)

Madoc: A Mystery (1990)

The Annals of Chile (1994)

Hay (1998)

Poems 1968-1998 (2001)

Moy Sand and Gravel (2002)

Horse Latitudes (2006)

The End of the Poem: Oxford Lectures (2006)

Maggot (2010)

THE WORD ON THE STREET

THE WORD ON THE STREET
ROCK LYRICS

PAUL MULDOON

FARRAR, STRAUS AND GIROUX • NEW YORK

Farrar, Straus and Giroux
18 West 18th Street, New York 10011

Printed in the United States of America
First edition, 2013

Library of Congress Cataloging-in-Publication Data
Muldoon, Paul.
    The word on the street : rock lyrics / Paul Muldoon. — 1st ed.
        p.   cm.
    ISBN 978-0-374-26108-5 (alk. paper)
    1. Title.

  PR6063.U367 W67 2013
  821'.914—dc23

                              2012012378

Designed by Adly Elewa

www.fsgbooks.com
www.twitter.com/fsgbooks · www.facebook.com/fsgbooks

10 9 8 7 6 5 4 3 2 1

For Paul and Leonard

CONTENTS

AZERBAIJAN 3

BADASS BLUES 6

BIG TWIST 9

BLACK BOX 11

CLEANING UP MY ACT 13

COMEBACK 16

DAYS OF YORE 20

DREAM TEAM 23

ELEPHANT ANTHEM 26

FEET OF CLAY 28

GO-TO GUY 31

GOOD LUCK WITH THAT 33

HEAD IN 34

I DON'T LOVE YOU ANYMORE 37

IT WON'T RING TRUE 39

viii

IT'S NEVER TOO LATE FOR ROCK 'N' ROLL 41

JERSEY FRESH 43

JEZEBEL WAS A JERSEY BELLE 45

JULIUS CAESAR WAS A PEOPLE PERSON 48

OVER YOU 51

OWLS TO ATHENS 53

PUT ME DOWN 56

SO LONG 58

ix

TAKING STOCK 60

TIN STAR 62

THE WORD ON THE STREET 64

WOULDN'T DO 67

YOU SAY YOU'RE JUST HANGING OUT (BUT I
KNOW YOU'RE JUST HANGING IN) 69

YOU'D BETTER THINK TWICE 71

THE YOUNGERS (BOB AND JOHN AND JIM AND COLE) 74

x

THE WORD ON THE STREET

AZERBAIJAN

It might take years
To win your heart
To grab a beer
Would be a start
But our drinking late
In T.B.'s bar
Put our first date
In Kandahar
Though it was right
By an air force base
I would take flight
Only in your embrace
Though it was right
By an air force base
Night after night
We'd close the place

I worked for years
In oil and gas
Our engineers

Once flew first-class
But the factory's
Run out of steam
They don't need me
On the sales team
The water's still
On the mill race
I take the pills
Only to slow my pace
The water's still
On the mill race
As for the mill
They'll close the place

When the right buyer comes along
They say it's going for a song

We've lived for years
In the same house
Our flame burned clear
Took long to douse
But we're moving on

To Godknowswhere

Azerbaijan

Is way up there

The house we bought

Through Morgan Chase

It's come to naught

Only this one suitcase

The house we bought

Through Morgan Chase

We never thought

They'd foreclose on the place

BADASS BLUES

That's Charlton Heston belching on
   the set
I guess he likes the stew
That's Charlton Heston belching on
   the set
Guess he likes the camel stew
Charlton Heston's belching on the set
Arnold Rothstein's welching on a bet
They've got them badass blues

Arnold Rothstein scored a dirty game
In his two-tone wing-tip shoes
Arnold Rothstein scored a dirty game
In his two-tone wing-tip shoes
Arnold Rothstein scored a dirty game
But T. S. Eliot wore the shirt of flame
They'd got them badass blues

T. S. Eliot simply never dared
To capitalize the "J" in Jew

T. S. Eliot simply never dared
To capitalize the "J" in Jew
T. S. Eliot simply never dared
To challenge Albert Einstein's E=MC^2
Thought they'd both got them badass
    blues

Albert Einstein looks vaguely like
    a dog
That's sacred to the Hindu
Albert Einstein looks vaguely like
    a dog
That's sacred to the Hindu
Albert Einstein looks vaguely like
    a dog
And Egypt is still plagued by frogs
They've got them badass blues

Egypt's cracking down on the
    malcontents
With their progressive views
Egypt's cracking down on the
    malcontents

With all their progressive views
While Egypt's cracking down on the
   malcontents
You and I are fighting over what Eddie
   Falcon meant
When he sang "The Young Have No
   Time to Lose"

Now Egypt's squelching the Internet
They've blacked out the news
Now Egypt's squelching the Internet
They've blacked out the news
Now Egypt's squelching the Internet
And Charlton Heston's belching on
   the set
They've sure got them badass blues

BIG TWIST

It turns out Planet of the Apes
Is our own planet Earth
The priceless Maltese Falcon
Has virtually no worth
All those statues and statuettes
Have proved a total sham
Though liberty had once seemed set
On winning the Grand Slam
Your falling for me that first day
Was the first clue I missed
And that you've loved me all along
Is clearly the big twist

It turns out that in Chinatown
Incest gives a fresh slant
To a retired Blade Runner's
Being a replicant
I'd guessed you must be cyber-born
Till you opened the dam
And wept to read a unicorn's

Last origami-gram
The thought I'm secretly your prey
Is one I've not dismissed
For that you've loved me all along
Is clearly the big twist

It turns out at the Bates Motel
Cross-dressing's the new fad
Princess Leia is Luke's sister
Darth Vader is their dad
A Starfighter has the Blue Book
Value of your Trans Am
The way you suck that bone you look
More and more like your mam
A galaxy far far away
Remains shrouded in mist
But that you've loved me all along
Is clearly the big twist

BLACK BOX

The men who dreamed up the
    airplane
We know they were next of kin
Wilbur Wright rounded out Orville
They came through thick and thin
An airplane flew low over your bed
Concocting itself as it flew
I don't know what happened along
    the way
To make me come up with you

The man who invented barbed wire
We know he was unrestrained
He loved a legal entanglement
He loved ground lost and gained
The barbed wire encircling your
    showerhead
Your rather contrived tattoo
I don't know what happened along
    the way
To make me come up with you

The man who hit on the black box
We know he did what he did
Because his dad died in a plane crash
When he was just a kid
The black box is often orange or red
That in itself is a clue
I don't know what happened along
the way
To make me come up with you
I don't know what happened along
the way
To make me come up with you

CLEANING UP MY ACT

There are no gentlemen
In a gentleman's club
A direct flight to Reno
May stop at a hub
I flagged behind my flagon
Of Côtes du Rhône
You'd passed out in the passion
  wagon
When I asked you home
I told you it's a condo
It's a cold-water flat
The tricks I've played are dirty tricks
That's why I'm cleaning up my act

Nothing is a problem
To a problem child
Though the issue of labeling
Sends me hog wild
I pick up the plot that thickens
Around a free-range pig

I check out a fresh chicken
To find it's been deep-chilled
When did you last hear a kettle
Call a kettle black?
I've been defiled by your sales pitch
That's why I'm cleaning up my act

For I was taken in
By the identical twin
Of a pole dancer from Denver my
   oh my
As for her skin
It was barely as thin
As the pretext under which she asked
   me why

There are no gentlemen
In a gentlemen's club
No room for nuclear families
In a nuclear sub
A flight may run from Reno
To a renal ward

14

A tall cappuccino

Turns out to be small

Many's a mass of sugar

Sells itself as low fat

I'm hoping to be filthy rich

That's why I'm cleaning up my act

COMEBACK

We were introduced by Bruce
At the Stone Pony
All that concentrated juice
Standing room only
You were with some suit
From EMI or Sony
Who was so full of toot
He called for "Mony Mony"
You came back to the slum
The squat with Lars and Sammy
Then Lanois's green thumb
Grew us a golden Grammy
And then our double album
Hit a double whammy
When it reached number one
We reached for our swami

To make a comeback baby
A comeback don't you see
It's time to come back baby
Come back baby to me

Then our master's voice
Told us it was cool
To park the Rolls-Royce
In the swimming pool
While our drugs of choice
Were run from Istanbul
Through a girl called Joyce
Whose real name was Mule
We loved the paparazzi flash
The paparazzi zoom
When we finished our stash
Of magic mushrooms   17
We'd pay in cash
For a kilo of Khartoum
And come back to trash
Another hotel room

And make a comeback baby
A comeback don't you see?
It's time to come back baby
Come back baby to me

When we broke up we swore we'd never
  kiss and tell
Never speak to each other until hell
Freezes over or whatever hell does
When it's co-produced by Eno and Was
But *Behind the Music* and *Where Are*
  They Now?
Have pointed the way they've shown
  us how
To take a leaf from Plant and Page
And Fleetwood Mac and set the stage

For a comeback baby
A comeback don't you see?
It's time to come back baby
Come back baby to me

We'd no sooner said farewell
Than it was time to reunite
A flame's likelier to swell
In a diminished light
For though we're a hard sell

What with the cellulite
We're still clear as a bell
We're still pretty tight
So let's remember the fans
As we fan the embers
And hit the Meadowlands
This coming September
When we take each other's hands
Baby let's remember
We're just another band
With only two surviving members

19

Making a comeback baby
From yet another rave
A comeback baby
A comeback from the grave

DAYS OF YORE

There's where Punch found Judy
Hanging with Howdy Doody
When Punch became quite moody
And engaged in fisticuffs
We know behind the wolf bully
Is a sheep with a pulley
And its arguments get woolly
When someone calls its bluff
You and I have been at daggers drawn
Since I watched *Duel of the Titans*
   next door
When we would have moved on
In days of yore

There's where Ian Dury
Was sentenced by a jury
For smelling like a brewery
Before he'd had a beer
It was only when a pencil shover
On *The Cook the Thief His Wife and*
   Her Lover

Removed the lens cover
Everything became quite clear
Rather than let things get out of
    hand
And declare an all-out war
Judy would have issued a mild
    reprimand
In days of yore

I know you think my tendency
To discuss swimming pools in
    Southend-on-Sea
With our neighbor Miss Descartes
Suggests that's not all we explore
We also discuss how a kid with polio
And a half-decent portfolio
Could get into the Royal College
    of Art
In those far-off days of yore

There's where Doctor Bungle
Mistook viral for fungal
And a "flaw of the jungle"

Became the missing link
We can trace Judy's strictures
To the time Punch drop-kicked her
And left her sound and picture
Slightly out of sync
Even if she'd been left
On the cutting-room floor
Judy would never have felt bereft
In days of yore

She'd have picked herself right up
And offered her breast to a wolf pup

DREAM TEAM

We used to be partners

Along the winding road

Lennon and McCartney

Ratty and Mr. Toad

Wyatt Earp and Dodge

The girl who's kinda miffed

At the hodgepodge

The Three Kings brought as gifts

A dog and its manger

Strawberries and cream

Tonto and the Lone Ranger

We were a dream

We were a dream

We were a dream team

We used to be buddies

In our college days

The spine and the shudder

The Mets and Willie Mays

The petard on which we're hoist

Otis and the lift
The girder and the joist
Working the graveyard shift
History and Hegel
The mote and the beam
Lox and a bagel
We were a dream
We were a dream
We were a dream team

Until our efforts to tough
It out of the rough
Became the stuff of nightmare
Until we came to believe with Mae
    West
Saving love yields no interest
When you're such a messed-up pair

As used to be partners
In another life
Lennon and McCartney
Lot and his wife

The unconscious and Freud

Stella and Dean Swift

Staring into the void

Before they're set adrift

Freude and *Schaden*

Munch and *The Scream*

The Genie and Aladdin

We were a dream

We were a dream

We were a dream team

25

ELEPHANT ANTHEM

The elephants have done a bunk
They've left on the late train
For when it comes to packing trunks
They're speedy in the main
And when it comes to skipping town
The elephants have got it down
To a fine art
They too refuse to act their age
And when they go on the rampage
They're off the chart
They still rely quite heavily on scent
For figuring out what it all meant

The elephants know project teams
Are good for rolling logs
You think I'm pushy and I seem
To treat people like cogs
Because push always comes to shove
The elephants go hand in glove
In single file

When the dust settled on our show
You had me thinking you might go
The extra mile
To where we'd find a spot to pitch
    our tent
And figure out what it all meant

The elephants are less disposed
To hard work now they've found
The Vineland Drive-In will stay
    closed
Until the spring comes around
The Vineland Drive-In has two
    screens
Where everything we've ever seen
Was at a slant
The elephants take in both sides
As each projects on its own hide
An elephant
They also see how little time we've
    spent
In figuring out what it all meant

FEET OF CLAY

I met Joan in Peace Studies
We soon became best buddies
Where evidence was weighed
In Yemen and Myanmar
We tried to raise the bar
At the barricades
Some took a course
On Shakespeare and Che
Some took a course
In smack and Special K
I got an A-
She got a straight A
I'd dragged my feet
My feet of clay
Feet of clay feet of clay
I dragged my feet of clay

Joan kept her appointment
With that fly in the ointment
A pimp wearing pomade
She tied herself in tape

And tried to escape
Her coke escapades
Some think that fate
Was Shakespeare's mainstay
Some think Sophocles
Wrote just one play
Oedipus at Colonus
Destined never to stray
It's hard to retreat
When you've got feet of clay
Feet of clay feet of clay
Retreat on feet of clay

It's hard to move too fast
Unless you're a rattlesnake
For when the die is cast
It's often no great shakes
You're doomed only to repeat
Kissing your idol's feet

Joan wouldn't acknowledge
The crack she dealt at college
Was weapons-grade

When she went into shock
Her whole apartment block
Was under a blockade
Some hope the hellhounds
Aren't heading their way
Some hope to remain
Above the fray
Like a flawed genius
In total disarray
Who hopes to fall on his feet
His feet of clay
Feet of clay his feet of clay
Fall on his feet of clay

GO-TO GUY

If you've spent the housekeeping

I'm guilty by default

If my wounds are weeping

They're crying out for salt

I'm your sugar daddy

When the Dow slumps

Your '89 Caddy

When you hit those "speed bumps"

When you need another stock to buy

When you need another trade to ply

When you need another stitch to tie

I'm your go-to guy

If your horses are restive

It's because of my horseplay

If my mood is festive

It's because you carried the day

Last night in the EQuad

With the mechanical mugwumps

At Starbucks or Pequod

Where you manned the pumps
When you need another sock in the eye
When you need another fish to fry
When you need a first mate to say aye
I'm your go-to guy

Aye-aye aye-aye aye-aye aye-aye
Aye-aye aye-aye aye-aye

Though I bring home the bacon
You're still high on the hog
If I feel forsaken
It's not that you've lain with a dog
I'm your Elizabeth Bowen
When the cat jumps
I'm your Leonard Cohen
When you're down in the dumps
When you need another lock to pry
When you need another kite to fly
When you need another hope to die
I'm your go-to guy

GOOD LUCK WITH THAT

When the Sumerians hit on the lyre
And the Egyptians the cat
And I told you my heart was on fire
You said good luck with that

When Biro sketched out the ballpoint
And Stetson the ten-gallon hat
And Charnley his replacement joint
You said good luck with that

When Levi Strauss dreamt up blue
  jeans
And Adams the baseball bat
And Pasteur his rabies vaccine
You said good luck with that

When Glidden patented barbed wire
And Yahweh tit for tat
And I told you my heart was on fire
You said good luck with that

HEAD IN

One night at CBGB
Would bring me back to earth
I met a girl named Phoebe
Who loved to bodysurf
She said it's not like it's a sin
To rise above the grunge
You gotta wallow there to win
You know you gotta plunge
Head in baby head in
Never mind the pain
You gotta head in baby
Before you head on out again

Her boyfriend was a biker
Who'd started his own sect
He'd done some time on Rikers
To get things all correct
The punch he threw was kinda thin
Kinda noncommittal
So when I took it on the chin

I crouched down a little
Head in baby head in
Never mind the pain
You gotta head in baby
Before you head on out again

Don't speak she said don't try to
    speak
As we pulled into the lot
Between Jiffy Lube and Pathmark
She was Employee of the Week
She said I'll let you use my spot   35
But only if you park
Head in baby head in
Never mind the pain
You gotta head in baby
Before you head on out again

And I've been in a quandary
Since she and I eloped
She's never done the laundry
Too busy watching soaps

She can't bear to meet the neighbors

Too much like Antabuse

She's not going into labor

She'll have to be induced

Head in baby head in

Never mind the pain

You gotta head in baby

Before you head on out again

I DON'T LOVE YOU ANYMORE

When you and I broke up
You made me feel sore
You gave me the rap
I'd wrecked our rapport
My integrity's impugned
You've left me shaken to the core
You don't have to be a genius
To see it's kinda inconvenient
To meet in a convenience store
When I don't love you anymore
I don't love you anymore

As for the little creep
Who's stuck in his oar
It's that Johnny Depp
You once claimed to deplore
When Captain Jack was marooned
He had rum and whiskey galore
You don't have to be a genius
To see the man who's come
    between us

Is nothing like a man-o'-war
Now I don't love you anymore
I don't love you anymore

Your latest text
Has cracked the door
On the chance an ex
Might still want to explore
Things to which we weren't attuned
Things we missed on the ocean floor
You don't have to be a genius
To see my sentence is so lenient
Compared to being set ashore
With someone I don't love anymore
Someone I don't love anymore

IT WON'T RING TRUE

Once your spray tan and my fake ID
Would take us anywhere we needed
　to be
In this world or the next
Now I've set aside my feelings
For the pain you've been revealing
In your most recent text
My pride is hard to swallow
And my promise overdue
But if a promise isn't hollow
You know it won't ring true

Your idea that I might take a plane
Through sleet and freezing rain
Is so vacuous
Don't forget the whopper
Buddy told the Big Bopper
About getting off the bus
Buddy had played the Apollo
To victorious reviews

But if a victory isn't hollow
You know it won't ring true

You said I was talking hot air
I was talking through my hat
I was striking the wrong chord
I was either sharp or flat
Someday I'll hit the right note
On a Martin D-42
If a guitar isn't hollow
You know it won't ring true

Once my fake ID and your spray tan
Were all we had in our retirement plan
Then you headed for the hills
There's a chance you'll reconsider
And go with the lowest bidder
And bend to my will
I never said I'd follow
Is my excuse to you
But if an excuse isn't hollow
You know it won't ring true

IT'S NEVER TOO LATE FOR ROCK 'N' ROLL

It may be too late to learn ancient
   Greek
Under a canopy of gnats
It may be too late to sail to
   Mozambique
With a psychotic cat
It may be too late to find a cure
Too late to save your soul

It may be too late to lose the heat
It may be too late to find your feet
It may be too late to draw a map
To the high desert of your heart
It may be too late to lose the poor
It's never too late for rock 'n' roll

It may be too late to dance like Fred
   Astaire
Or Michael Jackson come to that

It may be too late to climb the stair
And find the key under your mat
It may be too late to think that you're
Never too late for rock 'n' roll

We have to believe a couple of good
    thieves can still seize the day
We have to believe we can still clear
    the way
We have to believe we've found some
    common ground
We have to believe we have to believe
We can lose those last twenty pounds

JERSEY FRESH

A roadside stand
Off I-78
She offers the bounty
Of the Garden State
Tomatoes sweet corn
And as she reaches
To set them on the scale
A bag of peaches
Peeking through their mesh
Jersey fresh Jersey fresh

That was an age ago
When the night I spent
In the horse country
Was its own prefigurement
I think of Botticelli
When he juxtaposes
In the Sistine Chapel
The foundling Moses
With Jesus in the crèche
Jersey fresh Jersey fresh

Even Botticelli painted himself
Into some kind of corner
I've got ten screenplays on a shelf
At MGM and Warner
The only one the higher echelons
Came close to green-lighting was
  Jersey Fresh

That's why a roadside stand
Off I-78
In Hunterdon County
Comes to mind of late
That young girl
In riding breeches
And a fishnet blouse
That bag of peaches
Like the world made flesh
Jersey fresh Jersey fresh

JEZEBEL WAS A JERSEY BELLE

Delilah was a Delaware dame
So loyal and so true
She'd never entice me to play games
We couldn't both see through
Ilana was from Illinois
So easy in her skin
She wasn't at all double-dealing
Though she dealt heroin
As for Jezebel
She put her horse
Before the cartel
And the drug task force
Even the dogs in the street could tell
Jezebel was a Jersey belle

Miriam was a Michigan miss
So constant and so true
She'd never be a rebel or be remiss
In paying IOUs

Naomi was from Nevada
Her failures so bittersweet
She wasn't at all untrustworthy
Though she worked both sides of the
    street
As for Jezebel
When she bombed
It was antipersonnel
And wired to the intercom
Even the dogs in her street could tell
Jezebel was a Jersey belle

From the way she sucked on a pipe
Between classes at film school
She said one night in a fleabag motel
She thought I was swell
But she favored dissolves over wipes
As a general rule
Even the dogs in the street could tell
Jezebel was a Jersey belle

Rebecca was from Rhode Island right
So steadfast and so true

She'd never pull the noose so tight

As just when I withdrew

Tabitha was from Tennessee

Such lovely doelike eyes

She wasn't at all perfidious

Though she'd worked for the FBI

As for Jezebel

A wire would take root

Inside the lapel

Of her chalk-stripe suit

Even the dogs in the street could tell

Jezebel was a Jersey belle   47

JULIUS CAESAR WAS A PEOPLE PERSON

Julius Caesar was a people person
He knew how people felt
He knew it took a little coercion
When the people were the Celts
In a mountain pass he'd kick some ass
Then hightail it back to the gym
Till the top brass got fed up en masse
And had their knives out for him
He shrank from Brutus's mild
    aspersion
With an *Et tu, Brute, et tu*
Julius Caesar was a people person
A people person like you

Machiavelli was a people person
Whose ambition was quite huge
Yet he steered clear of the bold
    assertion

And went by subterfuge

He tried to convince any would-be
   prince

He must work behind the scenes

Though it made him wince it didn't
   matter since

The ends justify the means

He was always up for a little
   subversion

As in plotting a palace coup

Machiavelli was a people person

A people person like you   49

As I drove back from JFK

The day you left me for Bill

I recalled your expressing the vagary

That you adored Fresh Kills

Adolf Hitler and Saddam Hussein

They both loved a landfill

Saddam Hussein and Idi Amin

Both had your people skills

Joseph Stalin was a people person
He liked to put his stamp
On people he sent for an excursion
To some far-flung labor camp
Though he wondered why collectives
    wouldn't fly
He had no truck with self-doubt
Five years can go by in the blink of
    an eye
When there's no time to laze about
That's why he favored physical
    exertion
For the social parasite and Jew
Joseph Stalin was a people person
A people person like you

OVER YOU

The things they make in Trenton
Are taken by the world
You were made in Trenton
I took you for my girl
You'd broken up with Jesus
His voice was soft and low
He still hung between us
He and I would come to blows
Over you my darling over you
He and I would come to blows
Over you over you over you

He'd still strut that Stratocaster
Despite his broken arm
Your homemade white-flour plaster
Seemed to work a charm
After six months in Philly
Your face grew hard and small
Your look had turned so chilly
And loss was written all
Over you my darling over you

Loss was written all over you
Over you over you over you

I met Jesus in the Wawa
His hoodie still said Everlast
The little shit
He'd lost none of his swagger
His arm may have been in a cast
But you'd written your name on it
You'd written your name on it

Like I'd found you in flagrante
One rainy afternoon
Back in the years of plenty
The powder and the spoon
The gutter loves a downpour
The guitar loves a touch
I'd love to settle a score
Or two now that I'm pretty much
Over you my darling over you
Pretty much over you
Over you over you over you

OWLS TO ATHENS

I got how the McGuffin just kick-
    starts the plot
You're bringing owls to Athens
Giving me what I've got
I know she slept with Kevin at that
    last trade show
You're bringing owls to Athens
Telling me what I know

I got how I'd told her often I would
    change my spots
You're bringing owls to Athens
Giving me what I've got
I know how Jane Smith-Hyphen
    came as quite a blow
You're bringing owls to Athens
Telling me what I know

I got how her sense of grievance was
    bought as a job lot

You're bringing owls to Athens
Giving me what I've got
I know she kinda stiffens when we
    meet at the Mirabeau
You're bringing owls to Athens
Telling me what I know

I got how *Unforgiven* gave Clint
    another shot
You're bringing owls to Athens
Giving me what I've got
I know I'm still ravenous though I've
    eaten so much crow
You're bringing owls to Athens
Telling me what I know

I got how *Kingdom of Heaven* did it for
    Ridley Scott
You're bringing owls to Athens
Giving me what I've got
I know we're even stephen our ratings
    are so low

You're bringing owls to Athens
Telling me what I know

I got how Jane Smith-Hyphen kinda
   stirred the pot
You're bringing owls to Athens
Giving me what I've got
I know she too slept with Kevin at
   that last trade show
You're bringing owls to Athens
Telling me what I know

55

PUT ME DOWN

I want to be the transport ship
From which we both lift off
I want to be the cartridge clip
In your Kalashnikov
I want to play war games in which
We get to use live rounds
And though you've left me for dead in
  a ditch
At least you've put me down
Put me down put me down
At least you've put me down

I want to be the rifle butt
You hold close to your breast
I don't care if your comments cut
Right through my Kevlar vest
I want to be within your scope
Should your remarks rebound
I guess I'm still hoping against hope
You won't just put it down

Put it down put it down
You won't just put it down

To my being on tenterhooks
Whenever you're around
I want to be the instruction book
You simply can't put down
Put down my love put down
The manual you can't put down

I want to be the haversack
That hangs about your neck
I'd follow you to hell and back
From this same helideck
I want to be the smoke that clears
Above the battleground
When the cry goes up for volunteers
I trust you'll put me down
Put me down put me down
I trust you'll put me down

<u>SO LONG</u>

So long as you think Obama
Is an abomination
The first season of *St. Elsewhere*
Not worthy of devotion
Over takeout egg foo young
So long as you think Genghis Khan
Isn't your next of kin
And Maestro Itzhak Perlman
Should lose the violin
I'll be saying so long
So long I'll be saying so long

So long as you think venison
Is a form of stagflation
Or that the blind leading the blind
Are a couple of Venetians
Who've camped by a billabong
So long as you think Valley Girls
Must still be parking cars
Galileo giving it a whirl's

What had him seeing stars
I'll be saying so long so long
I'll be saying so long

So long so long so long so long
So long so long so long so long

So long as you think cannabis
Is the gateway to cannibalization
And a cold case of Sherlock Holmes
Means a 7 percent solution
And that's pretty strong   59
So long as you think a pink slip
Is what you give your crew
And your running a tight ship's
What's made me stick with you
I'll be saying so long
So long I'll be saying so long

TAKING STOCK

Your ancestors killed Vikings
But I harbor a liking
For the midnight raid
It still takes a village
If you want to rape and pillage
In the brokerage trade
You gave me an inflated sense of my
   worth
Then dumped me in a block
Ever since my bubble burst
You've left me taking stock

Once you drank skinny lattes
With his highness Joe Pilates
In the Burberry range
Then at dinner with some suits we
Found ourselves playing footsie
I don't mean the exchange
Suddenly the whole thing went to hell
I was washed up on the rocks

Ever since my index fell
You've left me taking stock

Your ancestors ran a rout
As mine put out to sea
With the gang from Bear Stearns
Let's hope things have bottomed out
For you and me
And there'll be some upturn

I was in such a panic
My strategy's nonorganic
Like when we took Iraq
You've been so persuasive
Your procedure's noninvasive
I haven't watched my back
Day after day the price of my shares
  is slashed
When the bell rings at four o'clock
Ever since the market crashed
You've left me taking stock

TIN STAR

I say I'll turn myself in
If you let me lie
Till a star of tin's
In the morning sky
If you let me lie
And do some other stuff
Till the morning sky
Calls the river's bluff
And enough's enough
Yeah enough's enough

I'd done that other stuff
So you and I split
You said enough's enough
Of that other shit
You and I split
So they'd lose our trail
All that other shit
In Aspen and Vail
But they were on our tail
They were on our tail

They might lose our trail
For a day or two
But they were on our tail
When green came to blue
After a day or two
You said Lee Van Cleef's
One green eye and one blue
Above his bandit kerchief
Kinda beggared belief
Kinda beggared belief

You say Mr. Van Cleef
Pinned you to his chest
And now it beggars belief
You'd take off your vest
For pinned to your breast
Is a star of tin
You say I'm under arrest
You've cocked your rolling pin
I say I'll turn myself in
I say I'll turn myself in

THE WORD ON THE STREET

It's still the party line
The official position
Everything's still fine
At Seventeenth and Mission
It's all still sweet
It's all hunky-dory
But the word on the street
That's another story
The word on the street
Is we're quitting
Now our course is run
The word on the street
Is you're splitting
The word on the street
Is we're done

When the news first broke
The conventional wisdom
Was they found no coke
In the cockatoo's system
All's still going a treat

We're just fine and dandy
But the word on the street
Is you're into nose candy
The word on the street
Is we've tasted
The scouring of the fleshpots
The word on the street
Is you're wasted
The word on the street
Is we're shot

The trooper must have stated that   65
    official position
When he pulled you over on Friday
    night
Even as he was charging you with
    possession
You insisted everything was
    shipshape despite

The rumors they might float
For the prevailing doctrine
Is still our little boat

Has a sturdy coxswain

All's trim and neat

We're just super-duper

But the word on the street

Is you tried to buy that trooper

The word on the street

Is no one's talking

Except maybe the cockatoo

It says the word on the street

Is you're walking

The word on the street

Is we're through

WOULDN'T DO

I want to take a hit
Of your XTC
I want my name in lights
Above your marquee
I won't call it quits
Till you fire an RIP
You answered my want ad
What you got was me
When it comes to finding ways
Of being close to you
There's almost nothing
I wouldn't do

I want to feel the rush
Of your PCP
I want to turn your lock
With my skeleton key
I won't be feeling flush
Till you're my WC
I've set my GPS

For the Girls' Preparatory
When it comes to finding ways
Of hanging out with you
There's almost nothing
I wouldn't do

To try to make you break
Your adultery taboo
Though you told me straight
It just wouldn't do

I want to drop a tab
Of your LSD
I want the grossest part
Of your GNP
I want cash on the nail
And bang for the buck
I want to harpoon a whale
For the neighborhood potluck
When it comes to finding ways
Of looking good to you
There's almost nothing
I wouldn't do

YOU SAY YOU'RE JUST HANGING OUT (BUT I KNOW YOU'RE JUST HANGING IN)

I wish you'd leave your one-bedroom
Fly back to me directly
Even a crow will not presume
To stick to the script exactly
You like to shoot straight from
  the hip
When you're pouring a drink
And tending bar brings in the tips
That pay for time to think
Your one-bedroom on Bleecker Street
Its bathtub full of gin
You say you're just hanging out
But I know you're just hanging in

I wish you'd lose at least one layer
Of your obstinacy
Even a mule's a team player
Though its desk's a lot less laden

Tonight Death Valley seems to run
From Bleecker to Broadway
You're hauling borax by the ton
While I pay and display
You look like your own winding sheet
Held up by two clothespins
You say you're just hanging out
But I know you're just hanging in

I wish you'd find a way to chill
Stop your exaggerations
Even a mole makes a molehill
Out of the nearest mountain
Your writing desk is barbed-wire
   fenced
It's you against the word
But that's not all you're up against
From everything I've heard
Your one-bedroom on Bleecker Street
Its walls are paper thin
You say you're just hanging out
But I know you're just hanging in

YOU'D BETTER THINK TWICE

If you go for a bit on the side

With Ruth on the Rescue Squad

I'm gonna claim you died

Because of an act of God

When it comes to the crunch

I'll have to disabuse

You of the notion a rabbit punch

Barely leaves a bruise

They'd better load up on ice

Down at First Response

You'd better think twice

'Cos you'll only two-time me once

Yeah you'd better think twice

'Cos you'll only two-time me once

If it turns out you're having a fling

With Harriet from Ace Hardware

You'll have your eye in a sling

You'll be back in Intensive Care

For it may be doing it yourself

Is the last thing you'll want to do
When you find yourself on the shelf
With the realization a screw
Is mostly a torture device
Devised in the Renaissance
You'd better think twice
'Cos you'll only two-time me once
Yeah you'd better think twice
'Cos you'll only two-time me once

Though there's nothing so totally
   heartwarming
As getting back together
After a storming tiff
I'm simply informing
You you'll be totally under the weather
If

You're tempted to start an affair
With Kathy the crossing guard
Don't be surprised if you get there
To find your way is barred

It could be the damage you sustain
Is in fact quite severe
Though her moonlighting's on the
    wane
Kathy's still at King Chandelier
Neither of you will look so nice
When you're strung up from a sconce
So you'd better think twice
'Cos you'll only two-time me once
Yeah you'd better think twice
'Cos you'll only two-time me once

THE YOUNGERS (BOB AND JOHN AND JIM AND COLE)

You never used
To think like this
This bathing in a bathing suit
At the gravel pit
Once we wrestled to no plan
But catch-as-catch-can
I must have missed what was amiss
Until you threw a shoot
And had me on the hip
You never used
To think like this
When we were on a roll
With the Youngers Bob and Cole
Bob and Cole Bob and Cole
The Youngers Bob and Cole

You never used
To talk like this
This passion for a passion fruit

To which you now admit
You never used to be a fan
Of the Fall of Man
I've learned the history of the hiss
From your boos and hoots
You signed up for the guilt trip
You never used
To talk like this
No word of damage control
From the Youngers John and Cole
John and Cole John and Cole
The Youngers John and Cole

Maybe it is a good look for you
The sackcloth and ashes
The hair shirt to the knee
But your hair shirt's by Miu Miu
Or some other designer who
   rehashes
Our idea of how it used to be

You never used
To act like this

This business of the business suit

It being remiss to reminisce

On how things ran

Before the hunting ban

Ruled out the riding boots

The snaffle bit

The little touch of the whip

You never used

To act like this

Till we were out on parole

With the Youngers Jim and Cole

Jim and Cole Jim and Cole

The Youngers Jim and Cole